Crossroads and Unholy Water

CRAB ORCHARD AWARD SERIES IN POETRY

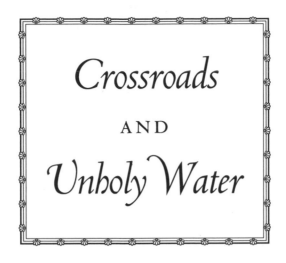

Crossroads

AND

Unholy Water

MARILENE PHIPPS

Crab Orchard Review

&

Southern Illinois University Press

CARBONDALE AND EDWARDSVILLE

The Crab Orchard Award Series in Poetry is a joint publishing venture
of Southern Illinois University Press and *Crab Orchard Review.*
This series has been made possible by the generous support of the
Office of the President of Southern Illinois University and the Office
of the Vice Chancellor for Academic Affairs and Provost at
Southern Illinois University Carbondale.

**Crab Orchard Award Series in Poetry Editor: Jon Tribble
Judge for 1999: Lucia Perillo**

Library of Congress Cataloging-in-Publication Data
Phipps, Marilene, 1950–
Crossroads and unholy water / Marilene Phipps.
p. cm. — (Crab Orchard award series in poetry)
I. Title. II. Series.
PS3566.H558C76 2000
811′.54—dc21   99-38613
ISBN 0-8093-2306-0 (pbk. : alk. paper)   CIP

For Michel

Surely every man stands as a mere breath!
Surely man goes about as a shadow!
Surely for nought are they in turmoil;
man heaps up and knows not who will gather!

And now, Lord, for what do I wait?
My hope is in thee.

—Psalm 39: 5–7

Contents

Special Acknowledgments

To the memory of my father, Delmar Phipps. And to my mother, Viviane Pauchet. Without them there is no life.

To my daughter, Valentine, who shows me living poetry, and to my brother, Gaëtan, who reminds me that we are notes from a divine song.

To my family and my friends, each one so uniquely necessary to the breath I draw every day.

Acknowledgments

I would like to thank the following anthologies and journals in which poems in this collection previously appeared:

Callaloo—"Haïtian Masks," "The Bull at Nan Souvenance" ("The Bull at Nan Souvnans"), and "My Life in Nérètte" ("My Life in Nerèt")

compost—"The Bull at Nan Souvenance" ("The Bull at Nan Souvnans")

Crab Orchard Review—"Marassa Spirits of Haïti" ("Marasa Spirits of Haïti"), "Caribbean Childhood," "Sunday Knife," and "Elzeer's Advice" ("Elzir's Advice")

International Quarterly—"Gaëtan," "Haïtian Masks," "Auxilia" ("Oksilya"), and "Dieudonne"

Ploughshares—"Ti Kikit" and "Caribbean Corpses"

River Styx—"Pink"

The Beacon Best of 1999: Creative Writing by Women and Men of All Colors (edited by Ntozake Shange)—"Pink"

The Grolier Poetry Prize ANNUAL for 1993—"Haïtian Masks," "Maneenee" ("Man Nini"), "Auxilia" ("Oksilya"), and "Dieudonne"

Sisters of Caliban, Poets of the Caribbean (edited by M. J. Fenwick)—"Out for Some Bread on Flatbush Ave." and "Maneenee" ("Man Nini")

I

*Caribbean
Beginnings*

Man Nini

Man Nini was queen of the coal kitchen,
standing within six square feet of soot,
in front of four pits glowing with embers,
churning the bubbling bean sauce, beaming

the yellow kernels of her smile at the chickens
flapping in the loose ashes below, strung
together by the feet with sisal,
their furious claws resembling the old

people's toe nails. She sighed as she sat
on a low straw chair, the heat-lacquered
columns of her black legs folded in a squat,
her soiled apron caught between her knees

forming a valley just below the wrinkled
mound of the belly, to sort out
peas, the good, the diseased, though all
grew round together in the same pod.

When she took off the flowered scarf she wore,
Man Nini's hair resembled rice paddies,
with traced avenues on her scalp that
glistened like the moist red earth

of Kenskoff Mountain in soft fog. The remnants
of frizzy white down were gathered
into inch-long, upright, puffed-up braids
which, in the darkness of the windowless

kitchen, seemed the luminous gathering
of her ancestors' will-o'-the-wisps, filled
with murmurs about the secrets of her strength,
joy, and the sweetness of the food she cooked.

Caribbean Childhood

I. Laundry

Hopping around
with a different sense of weight,
freshly cut bangs, uneven,
won't lie flat
except when pressed wet on my forehead,
at the pool where dragonflies
flirt all day with water,
touch and go,
buzzing like the heat.

The dog and I
on Saturdays would dispute
over freshly sorted laundry piles.
Feel the welcome of worn fabric.
Dig a soft trench. Fly a blouse-kite.
Drunk on smells of the family.

Then stealing down the stairs,
a sheet hidden under my skirt,
one specially fragrant with cares of the week.
Spread its whiteness over mowed grass.
Lie still. Feel alive.
The sun flashes
purple stars
in my closed eyelids.

II. Cotton Mattress

Seven years old and *insomnia*
means lying on a towel
covering a wet spot on the mattress.
A mosquito found its way

through the only hole in the net.
It drills into my narrow space.

Only yesterday I was sure
the Virgin appeared to me
clouded in blue and yellow mist.
The frogs, outside, had stopped their calls.
She smiled.

Dolls with painted cheeks
sprawled on my shelf—
they too stare into the night.
They wait for the afternoon dance
when I take them down.
Music is in my head.
Will the Gypsy dance
with the Mariachi or the Japanese?
Will they kiss quickly? I will wear
my yellow dress with white bears.
The black doll has no partner.

In the morning, Sentayis
will take my mattress out to dry.
He'll be mad but I'll follow him
anyway. I'll squat and wait close-by,
drowsy with the smell
of urine and cotton in the heat.
The sun will steal away
the spot I made.

III. Christian Girl

Before they dug a round swimming pool at the spot
where we would draw an altar with rocks, pebbles, red
and yellow hibiscus, Babette and I played there
at saying Mass, wrapped up in white sheets like robed nuns
with little Charlito as altar boy, to be

promoted to Priest only if he revealed where
he had buried all the blond angelical heads
of our decapitated dolls.

                    He never did.
Instead, at Mardi-Gras he handed me a box
full of newborn snakes. I used them all to frighten
my grandmother: "*LAMAYOT! DIS KOB! LAMAYOT!*"
I yelled, running down the alleyway to her red
front door dressed as a ghost (a variant of the white
sheets), "TEN CENTS!?" Smiling to the tradition, she paid—
blessed coins—to look in my box.

                    Come Sunday: black
patent shoes, white lace socks, white lace mantilla, I
had to kneel for my sins. The cross-sign of holy
water on my forehead felt wet for a long time
(I worried about the *bacteria* Charlito
told me would be wriggling on my skin). Ash Wednesday
brought relief: the cross-sign was traced with ashes.

IV. Water

Poolside . . .
Even the insistent tune of crickets
suddenly silenced.

My wet body on hot bricks,
face down, by the pool,
eyes clouded by warm vapors.
Water from my hair trickles down the neck,
feeds into a puddle
which cools my burning cheek.
Gentle splashes sprinkle
cold tickling drops along my legs.

I knew the movement of leaves above.
Stillness absorbed all sounds.
It felt good having a body then.

Outdoor Birthday Party—Father's Fortieth

Stars had gone to lie on the swimming pool. Tables
gleamed with white linen. Eight years old,
crouched on the second floor balcony, I see
when Oksilya sends the food from the kitchen:

Silver trays like musical notes
going down the mossy lines of garden stairs:
yellow brain *marinades*, fried plantains, *patates douces*,
red bean sauce, Congo beans, tomatoes stuffed with tuna,
white hearts of palm, coconut rice, turnips *gratiné*,
green avocados, breadfruit, watercress salad,
brown guinea-hen, beef *tasso*, pork *griots*,
pigeon, turkey, ham.
And Father laughed and laughed—Life looked so good!

Calabash trees paraded green fruits
along their brown arms the way ladies
wore rows of noisy bangles. Silver
glowed beneath their ears like on the underside
of *callimite* leaves ruffled by breeze.
Palm trees were coifed with a full moon.
Bougainvilleas? Orange! Purple! Pink!—
draping the side of the house and flung
over the roof—the colors of satin and taffeta dresses.
Women looked unveiled, fruit-laden. Men,
all the same: serious, shaved, lustful.

Desserts were brought down, all aglow
with candles—pineapple cake, *pain-patate* pudding,
coconut *blanc-manger*, chocolate-rum cake,
gâteau comparaîte, bananas *flambée*—Mother,
hibiscus corsage on *crêpe-de-chine* dress, red
round lips blowing a kiss from her hand,
entered the pool with an open umbrella.

Gaëtan

Little Gaëtan wanted our mother
to paint the walls black
so he would not see shadows.
Turn off the lights! She said.
But others . . . come too . . . he thought.
He slept with open eyes while snakes
crawled about his room all night long.
They fell from the moon's
gaping mouth and crept
through the cedar shutters
of the green window.

On starless nights, my brother now tells,
trailing shadows of people holding torches
came into the Mapou—sacred tree
with its root-ways mapping the earth
for an eerie city above ground
before plunging under
to a condensed breathless world.

He opens his arms to speak
of the Mapou spreading its mane, wide
and high into the firmament:
Who would guess at such turmoil inside?
Yes, ghosts of the dead and disappeared!
Devils! Fairies! They haunt the big tree!
And before dawn, go down the tide
of the wavy roots, away,
to wait again for the night.

Rain

Aunt Frances taught me how to rescue
drowning men. All shivering
from rum cocktails, she entered the pool
with her rubber daisies cap,
let her gawky body go limp. I hooked her
under the chin and struggled
with my catch to the nearest shore.
"Sometimes drowning men will fight,
and you have to knock them out!" she said
coming out of the water
to get another drink.

Sundays, kites were the kaleidoscopic
stars of the afternoon skies.
They plunged like red-tailed comets
into distant treetops, to be seen hanging
near ripening mangos, the moist wind
flapping through their loose discolored teeth.

Rain fell all at once.

A trap opened in the sky's floor,
poured its content in one throw
over us black people caught
in dusk's net. Rain ripped the soil,
poured gifts into the swollen river,
stolen gifts, skinned gifts—Aramis's pig
and Grasilya's three-year-old, last seen
playing in the cornfield by the ravine.

Rain drummed on the metal roof
over my pink bedroom where termites
by the hundreds lost their oblong wings
and wormed to their death

along the cracks of the old wooden floor.
Beetles attracted by the gas lamp
knocked and grilled their brown breasts
over its luminous ramparts. I heard them
buzzing long after I blew the lights out—
rain still falling—in their efforts
to lift from their backs, swirling dervishes
until silence overtook them,
from which a dust rag
would wipe them off early next morning.

Dieudonne

In Dieudonne's room, my finger
foraged in crumbling holes for small
matted balls of her own hair
placed there to attract protecting spirits.

Her bed exuded the unblossomed
smell of her life as Grandmother's
spinster maid. Her enormous breasts
hung above me, and she walked away
from my disbelieving glances, balancing
her weight gracefully. I shivered
before I climbed onto the straw chair
to investigate the faces. They were gathered

high in a single frame
beneath the screened-in vent.
Old and young faces she had arranged
in rows of six, passport photos
for trips they never took. Old and young
black faces of people who did not come to visit,
except a godchild sometimes, a girl
with large bows tight around stiff
braided pigtails, fanning out wide
like her skirt. She advanced shyly on skinny
legs, to kiss her childless aunt.

At Grandmother's house on Palm Sunday
I discovered, in the downstairs bathroom,
blood between my legs. I ran upstairs
to my mother. It is done, she said, I would
be fifteen soon and the time was right.
From the balcony she yelled out to my father
standing by the poinsettias, supervising

the building of a garden stairway.
Yes, he answered, after a long silence.

I missed the scented darkness in Dieudonne's old room,
her virgin body and selfish elation,
her black and white rows of waiting ancestors,
those for whom she did not yield.
I sat and stared. Obsessed.
I can bear a child. Pass on.
I am to pass.

Run for the River

I

Father has fought the river all his life.
It cracked his walls, dug its tongue in,
split them apart, sucked his land.

He built them again, stronger, thicker.
It bit his ramparts at their base,
spat lime-aged blocks several miles further down.

He dug deeper, lined up steel drums,
poured concrete over.
Now he sits with watchful eyes.

II

What's there for me to do?

I can't look at what's happening to the goat
Aramis was pulling to the alley behind
the coal kitchen. I have seen it done, there, before:

on its back, head loose, legs spread out (wings not meant to
fly), chest slashed open, ribs apart, organs pushing—
the goat, offered, blooming like a flower of meat.

Venant does not want me in her maid's room either.
She warns me: "Don't you sneak
in here behind my back! And don't you go
and bother your Mama, she is with her
friends! And don't you make any noise!
And don't you go swimming alone!
And don't you take your brother's bow and arrows!

You know you just nearly killed him with 'em.
And don't you go in the chicken coop
and get all dirty and I have more washing to do!
I don't have time to worry about you all the time.
And don't you make that face like nobody loves you
and run off to them hills alone!
I got no time to go looking for you
and Aramis got no time either."

III

Father!? I could go and talk to Father?
Well . . . he is sitting up there again, depressed,
with eyes as if he had been robbed.
Always he pleads: "sit a while with me . . .
His hand—knotty fingers and a gold
wristwatch—feels hard on my arm.
Is it always like that with families,
that everyone involved feels sacrificed?

IV

I know where to go! Down past the cherry tree—Ooh!
Full of cherries!—hop over the terraces
like I have Gulliver legs, down through the rows
of mahogany trees, watch for the low branches
of the tamarino, then around the corner
of one, two, three, the third dwarf coconut tree,
and, careful! Crouch and slide down the steep gravel slope
on my behind to the grass clearing; here I could run,
but, easy . . . lots of shit here!—
donkey shit, goat shit, people shit—
with garlands of greenish angry flies milking it.

V

There it is!! The arched metal door to the river!

Oh! The lushness of black river women
whose walking steps have bounce and leisure,
who travel down from sun-scorched hills,

splash their brightly colored plastic sandals
where water and sand get siphoned between their toes.
They sit near pools of brittle crystal

to wash soiled worn clothes,
their bared breasts reach over
and rest on stretch-marked bellies.

Marasa Spirits of Haïti

Maël! Four years old. Dancing!
All delight, dimples and dough!
                 Hungry!
Giggles as she sings for the Marasa spirits—
the infant twins—stumbles always on that *m*
which she turns into b, so she says:
Barasa men dlo men manje . . . —here water,
here food. The food part is what preoccupies Maël.
She supervises the ritual preparations,
her plump fingers fumbling into the pockets
of her lavender gingham dress, dislodging lint,
pinching cookie crumbs. Yes water, yes candles,
yes pale blue and pink flowers but
                          mostly sweets!
More, bring more! She checks their wrappings
as she counts them—she does not want the Marasa
to be short-changed, the way she feels at Easter
when the egg hunt leaves her
with less chocolate than her sisters.
Hands like open plates, displaying
and raising her small lot to my attention,
                    she cries:
the spirits need a full bag to begin the journey—
the road is long.

Oksilya

Lying in the darkness of sightless eyes,
Oksilya waits for company, tending every noise. I come
and find her in a buttonless gown, out of which one old
breast hangs. Oksilya our cook! Oksilya my childhood, Oksilya

with the smell of carrots and thyme from Kenskoff, dancing
a Banda in the kitchen, Oksilya buying me a pet chicken,
Oksilya of *corossol* ice cream on Sunday and daily glasses
of powdered milk, Oksilya my birthday cakes.
Oksilya walking on black and white floor tiles.
Oksilya of vacations in the mountains, shivering
on a floor mattress next to her little niece who played with me.
Oksilya with the laugh and the crooked knees, Oksilya!

I want your photograph,
I want to keep you,
do you remember me?
"How is the cherry tree?" she answers,
"how is the mango tree
right by the stairs
to the coal kitchen
out back? How is the orange
tree which gave bitter fruits
on the left and sweet
ones to the right for the morning
juice? Are they still there?"
"I did not know the trees," I mumbled.

"I am up! I am up!" she cries,
for all to come and see her walking
with my help on the way outside.
She checks her hair
with one trembling hand.
She lifts her head towards the sky.

Aunt Frances the Pianist

In the rough rivers where she swam,
Aunt Frances liked to anchor herself
with one hand to a rock, then wave
to us children lined up along the banks.
The water slapped and sucked
the unprotected parts of her body:

petals of rubber daisies on her cap
seemed like bouncing tentacles of one-eyed creatures
positioned in surveillance around her small head;
snorkel and mask channeled her sight and breath;
hard-meshed nylon cups held her breasts
within the bathing suit; black
flippers extended her bunioned toes.

Long-limbed, squared and no butt,
she waddled. No curves on her body
except for breasts which once had fed
her only son (born deaf) who spent his time
intent on solving mathematical equations
or reading out of stacks of comic books
about superheroes. She spoke little,
smiled often, but her teeth were false.

At night the teeth sat in a water-filled glass.
Her husband had his own bedroom. We found her
exotic, foreign . . . our American aunt!
(A noted pianist once!) . . . shy to show photos
of her parents' house, a sister, a cardinal
in a high tree, a field of wheat.
The only voice left from her home was her piano.

Her husband, the ears-nose-and-throat specialist,
always left the house when she played.
Music also made the two dogs howl
and howl continuously at her side,
every time, until she gave up playing.
For years the stilled piano remained
planted on the front room's green mosaic floor,
used as a table at Christmas
to display gifts. She drank.

For years. Rum cocktails
at noon. Rum cocktails
alone. Rum cocktails
always. In the bathroom,
thin towels were always damp;
tropical fungus blistered
the walls. And all the while
the dogs at her feet.
Scratching. Grunting.
Wheezing. Getting old.
Dying. Replaced
by the same.

The Gold Watch

"Just have it melted and make something else,"
my father said, giving me his gold watch.

He had taught me how to read time with it. We
sat close on the small open balcony
above the first floor, beneath
a mango tree's tallest branches.
His finger pointed to the thin gold hands
which make the passage easily from hour to hour.

One late afternoon, my grandmother died.
A skinny adolescent, I sat on my father's lap;
his balding head on my shoulder, he cried.
I can still feel his arms enclosing me
as if to hold someone who would never vanish.

In a way, he had also learnt about time
from his own father, the years when
he watched him, a white shape who lingered
every afternoon in the rocking chair,
unaware of sunlit flies swarming,
mourning himself, inviting silence.

Emma

"For You!" you'd say, with outstretched arms
offering me flowers cut short at the stem
you had been holding so tightly.
Your smile, a moon crescent
in a pastel sky at dusk.
Eyes brilliant from a contained giggle,
you'd disappear down the yellow hallway.

I miss your extravagance—
bangs over uncertain brown eyes,
little pudge by the armpits, lipstick
over pouting lips for a dress-up photograph,
your drawings of colorful dainty women
in high heels and high hairdos, the lice you brought
home from school and that horrible haircut,
a floppy hat to hide it, our chatting
after homework was done.

I see your naked body hopping in the rain,
shivering defiantly under the roof's downpour,
the orange door where I waited with dry towels.
I remember your lurking behind African violets
to watch me when I wanted privacy
and silence; I threw my sandals
at your forever-chattering-Christmas-present-parakeets
in their high-hung cage.

Now I have a house of my own.
I hooked a crucifix at the front door.
Every year's seasons are stations of the cross.
There is no soft blue bedroom here
like the one we once knew,
tulips standing on a marble tabletop
next to broken figurines glued back together.

Queen of the Meadow

I. Family House

The house was green and white.
Coconut trees fanned themselves
over the termite-hollowed balcony.
Thus eaten from within,
the house felt unstable.

Under the rafters, bats
huddled upside down.
Fearing for my hair,
I covered my head.

The mirror in the dining room
with its twisted gold frame
answered back the same
mistrustful look.

Mother wore green and lipstick.
She always cried for the bronze angel
we left in the other house,
the angel that pissed water
into the children's pool.
She glued cut-out flowers
from different fabrics
onto the walls and furniture.
She pasted her poetry all over the house
the way other people scrawl
graffiti in public toilets.

II. The Exiled

"Breath is so cold here," I feel,
"why am I so far from my beach-
skirted island where papayas grow?"

       Magnolias! Bougainvilleas! Hibiscus!
       Birds of Paradise! In the nights of my needs
       my mother exploded with colors and the scents
       of flowers. I thought: "Life's a parade!"

Her eyes are like birds that sit
on branches of a dry tree you pass
on a highway, a small dark accent
at the end of a sentence about longing.

I write her: "You are the most beautiful
of all that is beautiful."

III. Dogs

Followed by her eight howling, barking, growling dogs,
my mother runs towards me with arms
outstretched. Painted up like a formidable scarecrow,
her entire skin seems gathered and pinched upward
at the spot of her shrieking famished mouth,
like the cold wrinkled skin lifted from milk
previously boiled: "*Ma fille!* My child! My flesh!"

"You are always so stiff . . . you are not tender.
You don't know how to be a woman."
Oh yes . . . Mother. I do. I have
lain down, opened and spread out
like a secondhand manual.
My frustrated Furies have looked back
too often. They stalk my dreams.
I have frozen into dignity.

In her room, she clasps me close to her breast.
Her scent smothers me. I am an objet
in her private graveyard of muscular men
whose photographs are like inscribed headstones.

Each man has enlarged the emptiness in her.
She has been mined like a great hill.
"Promise me when I die you'll take care of my dogs?"
There is no thicket in my memory for hiding the other
truffle-sniffing hounds; all the salivating,
penis-protruding, vows-breaking "dogs" of her life.
Her throat is her body's dried-up well
where cavernous yearnings echo and die.
All dug up, disemboweled and deserted,
she is the graveyard. I
am the groundskeeper.

IV. Perennial Garden

I rest in a place of quiver—
the stage for your monologues.

> "You come from my belly!
> You should love me while I am
> still alive. You are lucky
> to have your mother. I wish I had
> mine . . . every night I dream of her.
> I wake up in a sweat, with a pain at my navel.
> She keeps coming down the stairs
> in our house, blond and tall.
> I am a child. I wait by her grand piano."

From the trees I learn that my voice
is only a hiss made by the wind
passing through.

"Feel the paper. Feel the handwriting
of your mother. It will stop soon enough.
You grew in me. Now you have gone.
Too far for me to imagine you
among your things. Tell me of your room.
Tell me of your husband. Did he get my photos?
Make me see the world from your eyes.
Why don't you write me? (I noticed,
by the way, you are losing your French . . .)
Tell me of simple things, the way I do.
My geranium has a blossom!
So red! So raw! Do you have plants?
My mother used to say that gardening
is a compensation for old ladies.
She was right. Besides,
Mothers are always right."

I am seeing a woman's body as it curved downward
towards the perennial garden she tends—
Beebalms, Honeysuckle and Colombines!
Obedience Physotegia! Blazing Star! Queen of the Meadow!

Life in Nerèt

Pigs and Wings

It's not the "oink, oink" you read about
in children's books but a claustrophobic
scream that pigs let out, with a sisal
rope pulling at their neck and cutting in—
nothing for their thirst, nothing
for their terror—even if what they lose
and leave behind is an imbedded smell
of piss, a mud hole which eroded their skin,
their piglets long gone, the only color around
is from the soiled spiral of an orange peel.

The chicken coop rots in the back corner
where, in days of my childhood, God, for me,
had a yellow beak, unblinking round eyes,
flapping red wings, and was willing
to hide and protect me, all tucked
and belly-down in the shit. Later on, when I sat
in churches, Saints also seemed powerful. I
wished, however, not for miracles but for angels' wings.
How much? Why here? How long?—
these questions I kept asking myself,
still do.

Sunday Knife

The clock outside the church of the Sacred Heart,
downtown Port-au-Prince, has shown ten of six for years.
No one cares. Time cannot be read. Here people

know what time is by feeling each other's faces.
Old women wearing yellowed lace mantillas,
afraid to be late for Mass, show up way too soon.

> *Tèk Raawww . . . Tèk Raawww . . . Tèk Raawww . . .*
> Jonas? Jonas? Ever been with a woman?
> *Tèk Raawww . . . Jonas! Can't you see I am talking to the bird?*
> *It's a Tako bird!, look, see its black and white tail,*
> *flashing there, in the banana leaves?*

> Zelya had just finished cleaning the place.
> She sat at the bar. Her large buttocks
> spreading over the stool seemed like shells
> shielding a red nut. Sunday afternoon
> was time off for the whores in Carrefour.
> Only reckless young mulattos would show up
> at this time, slam the door, feel Zelya's ass,
> demand salsa, bitches and booze!
> One of the three asked for a coke. "Such a honey-
> colored young fool," Zelya thought, "doesn't look
> right . . . too much moon in these eyes . . ."
> Only two of the girls could be found. Retired whore,
> old Zelya, cleaning lady, took Jonas by the hand.

Zelya was getting impatient. Jonas was still
immobile on top of her, in spite of all her wriggling.
She was about to shove him off when he spoke:
"I see . . . sex is like electronics! You just plug it in,
move up and down, the juice goes out of you!?"
"Yes! Yes! That's all." He did just that. It worked.

"You are a man now," Zelya said, "you should
have a wonderful life!" He was pleased.

By the stillness, Jonas knows it is Sunday.
Even his friend Sémi, the neighbor's cat, stays home
close to its family's kitchen to wait for scraps.
Jonas is invited nowhere. He circles
the garden, goes up and down stairways, holding
a little pocket knife in case he finds a fruit.
He picks up a stone to feel the moss. Catches
a tree frog, blows on its face to calm its heart.

He prays out loud for the sound of a voice, speaks
to a bird: *"You know moose? I love moose! Saw one once.
They kneel to drink water and seem to be praying:
they see blue sky behind their dark reflections."*

Ti Kikit

Ti Kikit puts on some pink lipstick,
stands on the Place Saint-Pierre in Pétionville.
For this evening she has borrowed a friend's
plastic barrettes, eleven of them, each pinching
a spongy braid at its base, dotting her head
with pink. She likes that corner
of the Choucoune Hotel—white bougainvilleas overflow
from behind the walls, make her feel pretty
while she waits. Her real name is Rose;
her aunt Asefi named her Ti Kikit
after the small brown bird. Aunt Asefi
was not really family but raised
her for eight years after the orphan appeared
on the road in front of her house.
Ti Kikit earned the small bird's name
when the thick rope she used to try hanging
herself left a gray scar around her neck.
It looks just like the bird's markings.

    Hey Bitch? Yea, you! How much you charge for it?!
Forty cents . . .
Wait here. Yea, there. We are coming for you!
OK forty cents! But for the four of us!
Ti Kikit tries to argue. They grab her
shoulders, push her down over the car trunk,
pull her short skirt up, bare her tiny ass.
The biggest boy shoves himself inside her.
The blood makes him see he is her first.

    Hey Bitch? remember, my name is François!
Ti Kikit's face is crushed on the windshield,
eyes dilated, white. She remembers Asefi's well
and Bourik, the mule, which tail-whipped
all day long black flies from its genitals
and from that raw spot on its back
the wooden saddle kept enlarging. One day

her aunt held her face, told her, "Be good"—
she could not take care of her anymore but
be good. Ti Kikit's mind goes to the one sheep her mother
ever owned, the day she gave it to the Spirits
as a last resort—its throat cut, blood
flowing in a tin plate, foaming, hurried.
Too many spirits to appease! Too much
hunger! Now these Mulattos are feeding
on her frail back. Gradually, her head
feels clouded and light, like the curtains
Asefi made for the house from old nylon slips.

My Life in Nerèt

Me too I'll have a child, me too I want a son!
Me too, me too . . . Ika is pregnant. She's my woman.
You know her, skinny sixteen, tough. We are dirt
poor in Nerèt. No running water in these slums.
Most people over there will kill
over water in the ravine: it's a trickle
and getting some is not like in America—
you get a ticket and wait in line.
Midday sun down there bakes your brains,
sweat blinds you, eyes stung pink like a Zombie's.
Ika's skirt's just a piece from a rag; her bucket
overflows with water, bathing
her face, makes it glow like new shoes.

Ika's proud! Pain does not stop her, just makes her more mad.
Five A.M., you see her going downhill
to the *Kwa-dè -Bosal* market, in town.
She sells roadside food: plantain, sweet potato, pork.
But neighbors have bought bad magic
against us—*Maji! Maji!* wherever you turn!
Thing is, the more we sell, the less money we have.
It's called *rale kob*—Ika's real mad! What does she do?—
Smashes all our wares, starts throwing
rocks at people's houses. Neighbors
all come out to defend their walls.

In no time, stones are flying like
bad birds in all directions. But
nothing can touch my happiness:
me too I'll have a son! I want a son! Me too!
We live in a one-room mud house!
Inside, I covered the walls from top to bottom;
all photos from a magazine *Madan Blan* gave
to my nephew Ogisten. That magazine's name

is *Nasyonal Jeografik.* Animals called
elephants! Tigers! Zebras, *m gen tout bèt*—I have
every animal! Even a big poster of a giraffe!
In there, it's Paradise! But, *Sezon la pli vini*—
come rainy season, this is what happens to us:
the stream down the ravine swells up like a river
with arms that pull everything down to its red mouth.
Soon the giraffe in our room has water up
to its neck. Our mattress is making its way
out the door. *Ika!? Ika!? Run! Water's washing
away all our things!* She is playing dominos
with our neighbor Pic-et-Coeur, a Rara gang chief;
he wears dark sunglasses even inside his room.

My son is born in Ogisten's red *tap-tap* bus.
He painted all the same animals I have on his bus.
His *tap-tap's* called *Merci Saint Yves.* Never made it
to the hospital. My son's whole life lasts two months—
diarrhea kills him. His life is washed away.
We watch him. Don't know what to do. *Me too, me too
I wanted my very own son—pitit gason mwen!*
Ika comes after me with two knives: *fout kaka!
Salopri! Sa w vin chache! M rayi w!!!*
It's in Nerèt she learnt to speak to me like that:
Worthless shit! She yells, *go back to your mother!
I hate your guts!!!* I hit her with a chair. That stops her!
Ika goes to her mirror, puts rouge on her cheeks, lipstick,
adjusts an old red wig on her head, slams the door,
walks up to the road with red high heel shoes, sits on
a milestone, back straight, hands posed on her knees, legs closed,
like a mermaid queen. She chooses to ignore me.

Pink

The *I Love New York* and silver heart
you see on my T-shirt is not
what I like most about it. It's the pink.
I don't know how to read and I may
not be pretty, but I can tell what looks good
on me. With my black skin, bright pink is it.

Every day, going home from work,
I walk by Jezila's stand at the corner
of Panaméricaine and Grégoire streets. Every day
I think "God I want that shirt!" But one day
I have three dollars in my pocket. Some woman
is bargaining for *my* T-shirt. I snatch it from her,
push all the money I own in Jezila's hand,
say I'll bring the remaining five later, walk away fast.

My husband has not found work for five years.
The minute he sees me, he grabs for the pink.
I grab back, run inside, lock myself in,
hide the shirt so he can never find it. He looked everywhere.
The children, he, and I live in just one room.
You'd think it'd be hard to hide anything? Not for me.

Next morning I walk out of the house wearing it.
He stops me. Holds me by the tits. He is pissed.
"Where was it?!" "I'm not telling! Not telling! Not telling!"
In the evening, my daughter hid in the room
to find out where I was stashing the shirt. "I know

where you put it! I am going to tell my
Daddy! I saw you sewing it inside his pillow!
I am going to tell unless I can wear it too!"
"Not if you don't want me to tear the eyes

out of that ugly face of yours!" I meant it.
You've got to know what's yours in life. Set
some limits. If you leave your stuff
out in the open, it's family that will rob you first.

Family Tree

Alone at my father's gate stands the peanut tree.
Burly branches spread over the land
and house where I grew up. At the tree's foot,
there is always some Zombie shit—
the size of an apple, red
with black dots like a ladybug.
The peanut tree was Lord. If you went
through the gate, didn't bow and say
to the tree "Good morning Master of the Land!"
your eyes and heart would feel closed,
you would not understand life around you.
The tree was the power of my family.
Neighbors respected us. Then
we left our homes to find work.
In the city no one knows anyone.
Men help themselves to girls like to fresh mangos
on a free stand. Just yesterday, I walked
to the Virgin's shrine in Turgeau. Imakila
was standing there, arms raised and wide open,
an empty gallon of oil in each hand, calling:

> *Imakile! Men mwen! Men mwen manman!*—
> Here I am! I am the one, I am
> the woman who bears your name!
> I came to tell you I can't
> take this life any more. Three days
> since I have had anything to eat!
> My stomach burns. In my horizon
> there is only darkness.
> Don't forget me! Every day finds me
> in this shrine, at your feet.
> Immaculate! I have a beautiful child!
> Not a cripple, not a face for Mardi-Gras,
> but an angel with all her fingers.

She is wasting away. Immaculate!
You know I love my child.
Yo voye tout sèvitè yo ale—
They dismissed all the servants.
No reasons, just GO!
M vle mouri!—I want to die! Take us away!
My family is lost. Six years since my mother died.
I am going crazy wanting to see my mother again!

That's what Imakila was asking the Virgin.
The sun rises before it sets. It should rise
for everybody, shouldn't it? Yet,
look at me also: my grandfather knew the tree,
my great-grandfather knew the tree,
many before them served the peanut tree—
poured rum, lit candles, pulled weeds—
still, my own husband is a good-for-nothing who
brings home his children with other women.
And I take them in. And they hate me.

Elzir's Advice

As soon as your husband is dead, slap him
and cross over his body three times!
This way you let him know you
are no longer friends. When he's in the coffin
sprinkle his body with sesame seeds and
attach lots of pins on his lapel. Spread more
sesame around his grave mixed with broken needles.
That'll give him something to do!—trying to thread
tiny seeds with broken needles—and
keep his mind off you.
                                        Wear red
panties and night shirt—they'll be like stop lights.
He won't be able to climb over you at night
(you don't want that, do you?).
Everybody here knows the dead have power.
He is bound to miss you. He was used
to your company—he'll want to visit.
Hell! He might want to take you with him!
At his funeral,
                        you've got to cry loud and clear!
You do not want to humiliate him—let people
know, by the way you cry, that he was
a good man, respectable and loved. That
is the only reason we are so noisy at funerals!
Not for the dead. Why, there is nothing to regret
about this earth!

Caribbean Corpses

for Allen Litowitz

Midday. The family sits behind Emmanuel's corpse.
His adolescent granddaughters, self-conscious,
their bursting nipples squeezed in white
Sunday dresses: three child brides for their grandfather's
funeral. Sweat gathers and tickles in the crease
behind their knees. A veil of mosquito netting
is spread over the body in the open casket.
On the wall above the coffin, a porcelain blond
Christ points to his own bleeding heart.

Green mildew lines swerve down Saint Peter's
whitewashed walls in Pétionville. Lizards copulate
behind the old Way of the Cross. One granddaughter
wants to keep this last image of her grandfather:
nose with folded wings which seemed to guard his face;
teeth long and yellowed, some old molars, rotting—
it's almost a relief his lips have now snapped shut.
Her eyes make out his hands—fingers like her father's,

who just happened to cast a glance at his mother
because his ex-wife—number two—is walking up
the aisle, dressed in white lace. Emmanuel's old bride had
already spotted her. Today she must mask
her joy at having won her son back since his divorce.
When she does not nag about his failed marriages,
she complains about his now dead father—she says
Emmanuel still masturbated at eighty-eight and
it's his own fault if he died. *Oui Maman,* her son says;
"the doctor thinks I starved him but it is not so."
Oui M'man; ". . . couldn't come to the table . . . has no strength . . .
a hypochondriac! It's his own damn fault!" *Oui M'man.*

Mosquitoes buzz in circle formation over sweaty scalps
of women smelling of too much Frangipani or Florida cologne.
Dressed in lace, satin, taffeta, they fan themselves
with one hand, slap flies with the other.
Men, in dark suits, repeatedly wipe their foreheads
and the back of their necks; so does the government's
representative sent to pay homage to the years
Emmanuel worked as a state civil engineer.
People searching the ceiling for air vents,
wondering who the hell planned this building like that,
find Saint Theresa's eyes are also looking up to
heaven while Saint Lucy carries hers on a plate.

Late, just off a plane from the U.S., Emmanuel's
daughter arrives at the portal. She enters
with a long wail. Her friends turn bored
and bloated eyes from either side of the aisle. She runs
to bury her face in her father's veil. Her mother's jealous
displeasure is distracted by a commotion
in the next chapel where a new widow
screams from the top of her lungs there is black magic
in this place, the Priest is a God-damn-
black-ass-Zombie-maker-husband-thief!
It's the wrong fucking corpse in the box.

Now something new is coming slowly down the aisle:
a white three-legged bitch with yellow eyes,
its head low, tail tucked close between the hind legs,
drooped tits brushing the mosaic floor. It pauses,
looks people briefly in the eyes, finally walks
up to where Emmanuel lies. A breeze almost
lifts the veil, but the dog drops a paw on it just
in time, pulls it all off into a pile, thinking
Ha! Human beings and their white veils! Give me a break . . .
Sits on it, yawns, scratches its fleas with a vengeance.

Out for Some Bread on Flatbush Ave.

With open lips like a gray rose,
a cloud hung over the church
of St. Rose of Lima in Miragoane.
Sunday Mass . . .

> *Damn! That day is right there*
> *in front of my eyes!*

         . . . our prayers
went to heaven. God . . . We were poor . . .
Faith was a stained-glass window blue in our eyes.

> *Where the hell is that bakery? I could die*
> *just looking for it!*

I could sing in those days!
I am sure my prayers went to heaven too . . .

> *FUCK YOU TOO,*
> *the sidewalk is for everybody, what's the problem?*
> *I SMELL MAYBE?!*

That fat priest really startled us:
"Would the family of the old woman
on the beach go out and get her!"

> *. . . NO! I am NOT talking to you.*
> *HEY! So what if I'm talking TO MYSELF! You don't*
> *like it? WHAT'S YOUR PROBLEM!? Shit . . .*

She had been gone for years.
With all this gelatinous green stuff and webs
of ocean mucus on her hair, undone,
her body, naked, my mother looked like
something the sea spat.

    Spat!

She had been underwater. People do.
And you don't have to wait till you are dead
to live in that cold world. *Voye mò anba dlo—*
send the dead under water—just for a while . . .
should have believed her in those days
when she took me to those ceremonies.
Ha! What difference? She still would have left us.
The family listened to Spirits then.
That's why she had gone underwater—
following a mermaid who beckoned to her, really?!
"The Spirits pulled me. It's because
they love me, they pulled me down.
I did not know I was down—everything
was the same, I saw houses, trees, roads, people
walking, eating bread, talking to each other.
The Spirits taught me how to make baths to heal,
I learnt all about spells . . . "

    OH SHIT! Sorry . . .
    what d'you mean CRAZY?! Fout LOUGAWOU!
    That's right LOUGAWOU! D' you look at yourself LATELY!?
    Goddamn WEREWOLF, get a comb in your OWN hair!

. . . Wish my mother had taught me a few spells.
Too many people, clean those streets,
Get rid of some population . . .

I COULD BLOW SOME NASTY POWDERS OVER THESE
New York streets, GET RID OF YOU PEOPLE!

For all these hours I spent listening to my mother,
what'd I learn?: "wash the stone the Spirits gave me,
don't you be sassy and disrespect it! Make
a bath with lots of flowers, basil, the kind
with large leaves and *monben fran* and *zo devan*
and lots of Florida cologne. When people come to me,
I will caress it, talk to it, and it will talk back."
Boy! Did I get scared the day I caressed it too,
and the wind whistled in the breadfruit tree . . .

> *Scared! Scared! And HUNGRY too!*
> *where the HELL is that bakery, where am I?*
> *YOU scary, YOU ugly, not me! LOUGAWOU!*
> *m pa pè w se moun ou ye—no, I'm not afraid,*
> *you people—you people, you too-goddamn-many people.*
> *My mother could take care of you people!*
> *A Manbo, yea, a MANBO! Nine years*
> *she spent under water, nine*
> *NINE GODDAMN YEARS!*

        . . . They pulled her down.
They pulled her down. Did she ask for it?
Pretty mermaid smiled. She wanted to get closer . . .
Pulled her down. And what about us?
And what about me?
Maybe that's why she was mad at them.
Still, she shouldn't have converted—"Jesus,
I only want to hear Jesus"—shouldn't have
ignored their warnings, shouldn't have. She'd still
be alive. Wouldn't have choked. Just like that . . .
wasn't even ill . . . Ooh I miss you Mama!
If you could see me now! I crossed over!
I was the lucky one. My roof is concrete
not coconut straw, I buy my food in supermarkets,

wrapped in cellophane, I stroll in underground malls.
Yet my body burns in this cold. Loneliness in a red coat.
But . . . I AM the lucky one. I crossed over . . .

NEW YORK!

This stretch of pavement is my gray beach.
Where is that bakery? Let me sit on my beach . . .
right here

HEY! Get your hands off me!
GOT A PROBLEM? What's your problem!

    . . . I close
my eyes to see a small pool I can enter,
find my body shoreless, at ease . . . breathe.
I undress to go home . . . be home . . . aah, that's better.
Gray sand is wet and cold. I close my eyes
to let my family come to me . . . I close
my eyes to shut out the voices, screams, sirens . . .
I close my eyes to feel my body,
come close, my arms,
close, my shoulders,
close, my face,
close, my home, touch
close, my mother, close . . . close . . .

III

Vigils

Keeping Vigil

Frogs were green, with a little red
when we smashed them against a stone wall,
and only a brown heap after
they had fallen below.

I could not go into the water
even if the big frog now no longer
terrorized the pool with
its scouting-round-glassy eyes,

so I kept vigil
over the raw guilty body
amid dusty pebbles and
trailing black ants.

Cousin Thérèse

Clocks, too many clocks,
                                ticking.
I would like back the first clock
my mother gave me, with gold vines
and torsades swerving like Thérèse's hair
about her face.
                "Go, go down deep . . ." —she lets
out of water-filled bags gold fish
into the backyard pond. They reach for the dark,
then resurface for a bubble of sun.

Cousin Thérèse helps people die.
                                At the hospice
she tells the sick how Jesus
stood in water to be baptized
before he could one day walk over it.
In small bouquets, she brings them daisies.
Petite, unfailing, feminine
                                she sits by the dying.
She knows them from their profiles—
horizontal, ashen traces, printed along
the white echoing strips of cotton sheets.

Which one has clutched her rope-braid
wanting to secure his descent?
How many hands have taken to their graves
the fragrance from her finger tips?
Whose eyes parched by the bland room
still stare at her on the windshield
while she drives home for supper?
Life moves to unexplained fragments
of music.

I miss the laughter
of the old woman who gave us candy
in a blue room overlooking the bay.
She told us those who do not pray
before sleep do not fly in their dreams.
From bullets, knives, or ropes around my neck,
I have lived many nightmare deaths my skin
remembers long after I awake.
"I can help you die too,"
                              she whispers to me.
Yes, Cousin Thérèse, I know,
with your smile only, you can make me
                                    plunge,

care not.

Waiting Room

Pain is a songless bird
pecking at the ears. An animal
which howls when the moon flares.
In the dampness. In the silence. In the night.
Where it whirls inside with
a breath that burns the skin.

Pain is why I sit here
in the waiting room,
doubting the day.

Pain is my mother singing in the garden
with a green scarf in her hair,
a bird-of-paradise flower on her shoulder.
Too beautiful. Too much to approach.
Too empty to leave me whole.
Pain is a child who banged her head
to sleep. In candlelight. And old
French songs on the brown radio
Grandmother gave away.

It is a friend's prayer at dusk
when his mourning doves were quiet
and these would not leave the opened cage
long after he was dead.
Pain is your face as you undressed
to seduce me; your eyes, pallid
when morning comes and you have fed
your passion to lingering ghosts.
Pain is missing your love
when you have too much pain
to have any love to give.

Two Letters

With scissors, she cut herself from the man
in the photograph. Just one hand is left
and part of his smile. This had been their most
beautiful photograph celebrating
their wedding engagement. His cheek gently
reached for her hair as one approaches white jasmine,
hesitant, awed, invited by its scent.
Seduced, he had smiled and the photograph
seemed to be telling a story other
than their life together had taught me.
Forty-three years went by between the artifice
of photography—love, at a standstill—
and the parched fingers, the striated nails,
which isolated the woman who glued herself
on a page and mailed it to me in a letter.

> He who wears on his face the missing part
> of the smile now writes from France:
> "just came from Deauville, I hurry to tell
> you, how I thought of your adolescence
> seeing once more this town, the immense beach,
> the area more handsome than before,
> enlarged with taste, Norman architecture
> preserved, and flowers! Even in this end
> of October. It was an enchanting
> *promenade*, but the weather has been cold
> and I am lonely. News of Haïti
> makes me anxious. Nine war ships still besiege
> my miserable country. I worry-
> where am I to go with what's left of life?!"

Frozen Feel

I. Stroke

The hand which had clutched the brake in the wrecked car,
later at the morgue rested over his heart,

> yellowed and gray, in the frozen last gesture
> of a sworn witness to an unspeakable sight.

He sees us now as he would have much preferred to—
from great heights and with the remoteness of birds:

> "Take all the Gods out of the temple,
> you must worship me alone!"

Parents are the true immortals. Bad parents too.
I think of the agave plant—stiff,

> proud and blistering with narrow thorns
> as it burst forth out of the vast lawn.

II. Passage

A little girl, soft-skinned

like a tree lizard, sits on her father's lap. She nestles

her head on his shoulder. Her long braid

eases down his arm. She follows the contour of his ear

with her thumb, supervises his face

with the satisfaction found in what has always been,

always will be.

Forty years later she sits in a church, looking

at his corpse, seeing his face—

now made-up—free from the white jaw strap

which, at the morgue was bow-tied over his head

like a limp Easter wrap. His features

seem the familiar garden where she grew up.

The frozen feel of his hand will be his last lesson to her.

III. Walks

At the time Father planted trees around our house
he said, "this land wants life!" I walked then
in yellow sandals over his newly terraced land.
Chubby, sturdy legs. Fleshy buttocks
like pomegranates swinging
with delight and determination while
the sea breeze added dust to my toes.

Years later, always anxious
during our silent walks at dusk,
he repeatedly pointed to the same
breadfruit tree, down by the river:
"right there, you will bury me."

Each time, now, that I walk to
my father's grave, what I recall first
is the glee of those children, when out of ribbons
from the discarded wreaths, they had braided
bandannas which floated and tailed far behind their heads.
They ran, looped and giggled
in a footloose frenzy whose aim was to dare,
touch the wooden cross and flee.

IV. Bone

It is not true
the dead live in
us. Seeing my father
stored at the morgue, I
now understand why
dogs will steal away with
bits of bone—tasted
treasures they hold
close in their jaws, can
dig up days later,
to sniff, lick, savour
all over again.

Haïtian Masks

I. Childhood

I thought that death had made him arrogant.
My mother had hung her father's
death mask where I had to look up high
to that hairless white plaster double,
the only face of his that now seems real,
sealed eyes, lips thin, tight.
High forehead leading to a rough dropping edge. No skull.
Surrounded by Mother's painted self-portraits
he seemed the rigid heart of a glitter-dappled corolla,
idealized, pained petals,
one of which was her gold-framed mirror.
There she scrutinized her paling face
twice a day, arching bright reds,
black lashes, geisha-like powder.
I grabbed that centerpiece
once for Mardi Gras
and ran with it
hearing mother trail after me with a distinctive howl.

II. Adolescence

for Guslé Villedrouin

Pour water on my head
so the sun might glimmer
on me. It is for hope that God
will pull them up by the hair to heaven
that Hare Krishna followers dance in the cold.

I saw my godfather's face
on the newspaper's front page, large,
written out as the rebel, caught
by the blue-vested Macoutes.
He had a new mustache.
I missed his gaze, deep chestnut.
Fat fingers gripped
his young man's hair
as if it were a big knot
at the top end of a loose rope, his neck
cut off.

III. Womanhood

for Yves Moniquet AKA Delta Acruz

You had fathered me into hope
after nested clawed creatures
gnawed at my heart.

I pull you from the moist shallows
of the bed. Your head
like a fading bouquet your two hands
hold at the throat
is offered on my lap, past use, past hope.
"I am afraid" you whisper with open eyes
in the early morning glare
when the parched burning in your lungs
sucks the last bit of breath
from your recurved tongue.

Now, I move through moon-blanched visions.
Fervor has the color of alizarin for a gravedigger
who wants to keep you from being thrown
into the communal hell-hole of those too damn poor
to afford a little plot of eternal peace
in the crowded downtown cemetery.
I come to get you out, reclaim you,

you, for many months, furrowed in the grave.
I am greeted
by another face
and a smile without lips.
A soundless wave of gleam-corseted cockroaches
scurries down the two sides of your coffin.
Through weeds, they run away with your image.

Old, Useless and Ugly

"Old, useless and ugly . . .
old, useless and ugly . . ."
she mumbles as she hurries to the place
she knows she has to reach or she'll die
from her heart she calls *the lead butterfly*
in my breast. "Old, useless and ugly . . ."
Her skinny legs and swollen, arthritic knees
under a flowered skirt speed down
the endless flight of stairs with a panic
like fingers running down a piano,
each step like a note getting deeper—
a sinking, a drowning, a choking.
Tears down her face, sweat down her chest,
big, blue, ceramic bead necklace bouncing
on her breast with every step down adding
to the beating her old heart is taking.

"Never wants to see
my ugly face ever
again. He should take
a good look at his
own. Seventy years
old and I have to
live with that!
He'll skin me
alive. He will. My
own son! For forty
dollars I can't lend
him he grabs me
by the throat?! *you've*
been greedy for life
long enough! I carried
him nine months in my
flesh, and then forty-five

years like a cross
on my back. On my
knees I scrubbed
the floor for that child.
I prayed, I protected, I
fought. I washed, I cooked, I lied.
I never gave
up on him dear
God! *You've killed*
my life, he says
nothing
good ever flies
my way. Where
is my blood! When
is my turn coming!
I wish you had
died instead of
my father . . . What
did I do to deserve
to hear that? How
alone does one have
to feel for the devil
to be content? It is not
God's name we
should not speak,
it is love's . . . "

Her dogs always wait for her. Still mumbling
to herself she opens the gate,
enters, slumps to the ground, limp
and washed pale. The dogs don't believe
their luck!—Thirteen of them—They jump,
hump and wag, each pushing, biting
the other to get closer to her face. They
yelp, yodel and gasp, God
they are glad to see her!
She is the light, the land, the sugar.

They snatch a slurp at every bit of skin
of her they can reach. Thirteen red and hungry
dog tongues of worship lick off the mascara,
the rouge, face powder, lipstick. Their saliva
enters and drenches her pores like new words
to redefine her face for her.

Blue Amani

There was no need for God to make people!
Why? Just so we can see each other die?
Wait here so teeth can rot, eyes go blind,
old age eat you alive. My mother died
with her eyes looking into mine. Seemed like
the rest of my life died with her then.

                                        Amani!

Sweet Mother Amani! You should not have left
any part of me behind! My life is a long wake
through which I have to sit. What difference
does it make if I live or not!? I'll go with you!

All my life, you stayed right by my side.
You did not let me come to Port-au-Prince alone.
But when you knew death was coming, Mother Amani,
you asked me to take you back to Les Cayes, that country-town
where your life started. You raised us there too—three boys!—
selling vegetables you grew on a scrap of land. Three
different fathers we have. They got you pregnant and, bye!

                                                    Now,

there you were on that little cotton mattress,
asking me if all your things are ready!
I showed you the blue dress—your favorite color—
I picked out at the funerary clothing store
near the *Plas Katedral.* You liked the dress
with its blue buttons running the whole length in the front.
You liked the blue slip, the blue shoes. Only the stockings
were gray—those are the ones the dead wear.
With my own money, I bought you a many colored
crown of flowers to please all your *Lwa*—the Spirits,
you know . . . You cried. Silently. Tears streamed
down both cheeks. Me?

                    I stand still, my heart breaking.

At dawn, I was there when you woke up.
You looked at me a long while, then briefly raised your
shoulders, dropped them, offered me your hands, palms up,
as if some truth was written there, water slipped
out gently from your eyes.

                        She died.

We did the wake in the evening. Buried her
the next day. Did not put her in the morgue.
I never want my mother in the morgue!
For the two more weeks I stayed down south, I slept
in the very same bed she had died in. She told me
"I won't hurt you if you sleep in my bed."

The sheets smelled delicious: she had wanted
to die clean. I was the only one she allowed
to wash her. A bath with twenty-one different leaves!
Every *Lwa* found its favorite in there too! I rubbed mint
and basil, *kapab, monben, laryèt,* all the good ones!
While she lingered in it, she whispered a lullaby. She looked
like a green water spirit! Odd bits of leaves, shaped like
butterfly wings, flaked off her hair and face.
I poured perfume in the bath:

                      Beautiful Amani! *Manman!*

I want you always
to be known in eternity
by your fragrance!

The Bull at Nan Souvnans

I

He was brought in yesterday
as an offering
for today's Easter Sunday rites,
pulled by a rope
to these ancient and sacred grounds of Souvnans,
then tied by the acacia tree, all day, unfed.

Now, noontime, he lies and waits.
His root-like legs make dust enclaves
next to his sweat-furrowed flank.
He no longer shows annoyance
towards the scrawny chick hopping
around and pecking at his flesh.

*"PA MANYEN L
SE LANMÒ W AP GADE!—*
DON'T TOUCH HIM!"—
a voice threatens us—
"It is death you're seeing!"

The bull stands up.
His nostrils reach, breathe in
towards the growing crowd.
Hands with a purpose, now, untie him,
take him to another tree. He goes,
as if for his familiar fields.
"DON'T TOUCH HIM!
DON'T YOU KNOW!?"

II

                    Now the bull is resisting!
              All legs stiffened,
         he won't get close to
      this tree! Swiftly,
ropes are wound at the base of
each of his horns,
                    crossed
on his forehead,
                    and yanked
on either side.

                    They force the flat part of his broad face
                    against the tree trunk.

                    Men dragging at his tail keep him
                    aligned. He can't move.
                    He can't see beyond the tree bark,
                    the roots or his hoofs.
                    Midday sun stings him.
                    A man straddles him, he can't move.
                    He hears all
                    where he can no longer look.

The bull trembles.
The ropes are tugged tighter
and fastened behind the tree.
A shiver vibrates down his spine,
his entrails deliver their moist soil—
he defecates. Someone in the crowd . . . laughs.

"METE GASON SOU NOU!—
WE MUST BE VIRILE!" Rene—
Master of Ceremony—calls out,
flourishing his machete
to the *ounsi*—handmaidens of the Gods—
gathered around him in white dresses.
They respond and wave their machetes,
symbolic wooden ones. Now Rene
shakes hands with the executioner
over the stilled body of the bull.
"LET US BE MEN!"

III

The dagger and the screams
start in the same instant.
Deep, long, helpless bellows;
thick, gray tongue extended,
recurved, stiff and drooling.

The knife misses its aim
　　　for the spine, at the base of the neck,
　　　　　pulls out and stabs again.
Again, twists, pulls out and stabs again.

Blood gurgles, gushes out,
　　　drawing a red web on the bull's back
　　　　　like lava's hands about to blanket
the city in silence.

The legs falter
　　　then regroup.
　　　　　The dagger thumps down again.
Again, the legs falter and fold.

Like a great ship sinking,
        the rear lowers first—his head
                being stuck at the tree.
But he stands up again!

"TO THE THROAT!" Rene shouts.
        The executioner abandons
                the spot above, to start
cutting, with a small knife,

into the thick of the throat
        underneath, inching the blade
                through the feeling flesh, alive.
The wind and the bellows

wrestle into the leaves
        above us. More warm dung drops
                to the ground. The vocal cords
get cut. A last gurgling hiss . . .

He can no longer voice what he feels.
Shut in. Further removed.
Hung by the horns, the great
black body slumps and kneels
to the live tree. The last
that the bull sees is not
this immaterial blue,
a tropical Easter Sunday sky,
but his own red blood's swamps.

The crowd cheers.

Haïti, April 1993

Niska and the Snake

... honey you are a dead duck! You can do all
the glou glou glou under water you want
and look at me with those yellow
bald beady eyes of yours, I am not
going to take my foot off that brick crushing
your back, I am keeping it until you choke.
I have been watching your slinky slithering
around my pond for a while. My goldfish are not
up for grabs and at three-for-ten-dollars I paid
I wasn't buying you lunch with those ritzy tadpoles
of mine you have been keeping an eye on while
they've been doing their job keeping an eye
on the bottom of the pond to clean it. This here is
my piece of tropical dreamland—my white hyacinths, my
purple peckerels, my water lilies and my
yellow irises. Babe, I'm gonna weed you out of my
grass! Your name may be Water Moccasin and you think
this water's for your roaming but my name
ain't Eve. I know your kind! All Cottonmouth
that you may be, you're not gonna sweet-talk me
or frighten me out of this Paradise.

                                                 It's happened
to me, once before, and I was just a child.
Haïti! That really was the Garden of Eden
for me, until same kind of snake you look like—soft talk,
loves the poor, justice, democracy, great
promises and all—skinned, choked, beheaded
all the goldfish he could catch, terrorized
all the tadpoles left behind. That cottonmouth
snake could have made a difference,
but like all the others after him,

he just went for the best catch, ate his fill, fat
in the sun. Ain't life sweet after all! Well,
I am not about to forget the way my brothers and I
left home and childhood behind: "wake up . . . Mother? . . . hush. . . .
put this on . . . why? . . . hush! . . . cover your face . . . hold this tight . . .
get to the car, hurry! . . . where are we going? . . . keep your heads down . . .
we're there, get out now . . . where are we? . . . quiet! . . . quick . . . go up the
plane . . . why? . . . move! They are looking for us, same who killed your father . . .
why? . . . to kill us . . . are we coming back someday? . . . no . . . never? . . . no.
Good-bye all, I'll be gone when you wake . . . family . . . cousins . . .
all sleeping . . . don't know we are no longer there. Good-bye
Granmanman and Grandpère! Good-bye Garden and Calabash tree! . . ."
Ha! Grandmother in the pool looked like a big mother frog sitting
on a navy blue lily pad, with the skirt of her bathing suit
floating around her waist and belly. Not a wild swimmer—
absentmindedly kicking her short legs
back, her wide breasts looking like eyes scouting
for her kiddies. All that's now . . . gone!

                              So you see, snake?
What's happening to you, I learnt from your kind.
It's been a long trip for me until I meet you
here—Guadeloupe, Puerto Rico, France, Texas, Alabama—
but I am not running any more! My own kids
are grown and I'm going to be a Grandma. This
Florida pond is mine! I am now a Southern gal in a
hell of a mood, who thinks you are taking your sweet, long
time to croak, my husband is gonna be home
soon, I've got to fix his dinner
and he won't find me here, a foot on-a-brick-
on-your-back, a foot on the shore, so I am
picking up another brick . . . here . . . and this stick
in my left hand I slip under your sorry belly . . . right here . . .

I just loosen my foot, a bit . . . that's right . . . and you
    just wiggle
      a little bit
        from under
          the brick on
            your back, and
              that other one
                in my right hand
                  is fixing to land
                    on you just as
                      you try running
                        away in the grass—
                          and I already told
                            ya I'm gonna weed
                              ya out of my grass—
                                you're doing great . . .
                                  OK . . . try to wiggle out
                                    a little . . . more . . . and
                                      my stick is going to flip . . .
                                        you out onto the grass . . .
                                          look at me all you want . . . I
                                            am still going to do it. . . . there
                                              we go . . . FLIP! . . . YES! . . . run, run, run . . .
                                                WHAM!

GOTCHA.